USING FORGIVENESS AS A WEAPON OF WARFARE

SHIRLEY VINSON

DMI PUBLISHING HOUSE
HAMPTON

Copyright © 2014 - Shirley Vinson

All rights reserved. This book is protected by the copyright laws of the United States of America. This book may not be copied or reprinted for commercial gain or profit. The use of quotations or occasional page copying for personal or group study is permitted and encouraged. Permission will be granted upon request.

Unless otherwise identified, Scripture quotations are from the King James Version. Copyright © 1982 by Thomas Nelson, Inc. Used by permission. All rights reserved.

Take note that the name satan and related names are not capitalized. We choose not to acknowledge him, even to the point of violating grammatical rules.

Cover Design: Tia W. Cooke

Library of Congress Control Number: 2014952906
ISBN 978-0-692-30523-2

DMI Publishing House
(a division of Dominion Media International, LLC)
P. O. Box 101
Windsor, VA 23487
www.dominionmediainternational.com

Printed in the United States of America.

DEDICATION

I dedicate this book to two people. The first is my late pastor Philemon A. Samuels. Thank you for the depth and level of teaching that you imparted to me. Thank you for understanding the anointing of God in my life and having respect for it. You saw this day coming and you spoke of it. I wish you were here to celebrate this milestone with me. You were a vanguard leader and a good friend. Thank you, pastor!

To Marilyn Janet Brown. You once told me that I was cheating the Body of Christ by not sharing my teaching gift. That one statement planted a seed that has grown to this appointed time. Remembering what you said to me helped to give me the courage to do this. I hope it blesses you richly.

ACKNOWLEDGMENTS

I would first like to thank God for three people who are with Him now in Glory.

Thank you, Pastor Moses Caldwell. I always said that you knew how to lay a strong foundation that would last a lifetime. You took the time to plant seeds in a little girl that would grow one day into a great ministry. You made church fun and easy to understand. I miss you so much.

Thank you, Pastor Bertha Rankin. I was drawn to you the first time I heard you teach. I did not know at the time that you were assigned to not only birth a ministry in me, but a teaching ministry that will impact the Body of Christ, and be a tool to win souls to Christ. You always taught me that "sinners deserve the best!" I promise that I will give my best at all times, just like you taught me. You were a wonderful mentor, Mother.

Thank you, Pastor P. A. Samuels. No one has had the impact on my life that you had. It was with you that my teaching gift was discovered. It was with you that my ministry reached another level. It was with you that I learned about destiny and purpose. You were the first to say the words "marketplace ministry" to me. You made me understand the assignment I have. You taught me to be a "HOW TO" preacher, not just an "OUGHT TO" preacher.

I would like to thank Dr. Sharon Jackson. Bishop T. D. Jakes says that in everyone's circle there are confidantes, comrades, and constituents. Girl, I believe you are some of all three. I am grateful for your friendship, no... your sisterhood. You're a great role model. I'm glad that I have you on this journey with me.

I would like to thank Lester Thompson. God used you to open the door for me to teach for the first time at Goodwill Baptist Church. I don't know why you asked, but because you asked, it opened a whole new phase of ministry to me. Before you asked me to teach Sunday School, I was content to be an Evangelist. I am so grateful that you saw the teacher.

Finally, to my Pastor Gloria Samuels. God has used you to launch this ministry in the direction that He always intended. I will never forget the day you looked at me and said, "You have been taught. Now do what you have been taught." It cannot be easy to carry on a legacy, but you are, and you are doing it well. God is pleased. P. A. would be proud. I am happy. Do you woman of God. It's working.

TABLE OF CONTENTS

Foreword   11
Pastor Gloria M. Samuels

A Word from the Author   13

Introduction   15

Chapter One   17
Forgiveness Has a Boomerang Effect

Chapter Two   25
Forgiveness is a Matter of the Heart

Chapter Three   39
Don't Take Things So Personally... God Already Does

Chapter Four   51
Why is Forgiveness So Hard?

Chapter Five   57
God Has Forgiven You. Now You Must Forgive Yourself.

FOREWORD

While reading this book, I truly thought about the person writing it. It is a different person from years ago. I think it's amazing how life lessons change us for the better if we let them. You can truly see this in this book.

The subject of forgiveness is explored to another degree and is well worth the read. This author shares the lesson that many need to hear if they are ever going to have peace in their lives. I recommend that this book become a tool to be used at book clubs, Bible studies, workshops, seminars, conferences and beyond. Hear the author's passion, pain, and progress as you journey through the pages of this book.

This read may just save you or someone you love from years of unresolved pain and frustration. It just may change your life.

Pastor Gloria M. Samuels

A WORD FROM THE AUTHOR

At the beginning of 2012, God spoke to me and said that it is necessary that He raise up some voices after the order of John the Baptist. He said that He is soon to come and that He is going to speak a word through these voices to prepare the Body of Christ for His return.

He said that the voices that have been speaking have done well. They were necessary for the Body to learn and understand how to obtain and live a prosperous life on the earth. However, because His return is so eminent, it is now expedient that He speaks words that will enlighten and teach the Body how to apply and embrace kingdom principles that will transform Her (the Body of Christ) into His bride.

Knowing that Christ is soon to come, the devil has intensified his attacks on the children of God. But we know we have the victory. God said not to be so concerned with attacks that come from without, but rather make sure that the spirit man within you is fully dressed in the whole armor of God and that you know how to use the weapons of your warfare.

The purpose of this book is to teach the Body of Christ the importance of using forgiveness as a weapon of warfare against the devil. As you read, it is my hope that your spirit man will become enlightened as to how the gates of hell cannot possibly prevail against the spirit of forgiveness; that you will become motivated to forgive those who have hurt and offended you; and that you experience a fresh anointing from the Lord our God as you move closer to His perfect will.

INTRODUCTION

Unfortunately, there is a lying devil who challenges us on every aspect of our lives. He uses whatever and whoever will surrender to him to fulfill his demonic assignments; and therefore we find ourselves in a constant spiritual fight. Satan knows and understands the weakness of flesh. Why wouldn't he, after all he controls it. He understands how susceptible we are to sin. He is well aware that flesh has no redeeming qualities. He knows it will never inherit the kingdom of God. It will never be able to please God or give Him glory. He knows that flesh will always embrace everything that God hates and that God will never have any fellowship or come to any compromise with it. God declares that flesh must die, and that we must crucify it ourselves. The more we crucify our flesh the stronger our spirit man becomes. The challenge is that satan knows well how to appeal to our flesh. He has studied each of us and he knows what we like and to what we are likely to succumb. And so we wrestle with what is right before the Lord and what feels good to our flesh. And this is the battle!

God understands the challenges of our warfare and He has given us proper weapons and the strategies as to how to use them. In Second Corinthians 10:4-6 the Bible tells us that the weapons of our warfare are not carnal. This means that our weaponry is not bodily, or crude, or tangible, or unspiritual, but that these weapons are mighty, meaning that they have a strength that can pull down strongholds. The church, in this 21st century, must learn how to fight and who to fight. Yes, we are more than conquerors through Jesus Christ. Yes, it is true that we have complete power over the devil. However, though these declarations are true, we must admit that there are strongholds in the Body that we must learn how to pull down. God has given us powerful weapons in our spiritual arsenal that can destroy the works of the devil, yet the Body is stumbling over the very principles it needs to apply to have victory. We have many weapons available to us that the devil's power cannot defeat. We may not think of them as weapons but they are. This book will examine one of these weapons. It is the weapon of "forgiveness."

Webster defines *forgiveness* this way: *to cease to feel resentment against on account of a wrong committed; or a pardon for a trespass or debt.*

Throughout the scriptures the Word of God teaches us that forgiveness is not an option but a command! To be in a state that you refuse to forgive or that you feel that you cannot forgive is to be in a place where you willfully ignore the will of God, and willfully embrace the desires of the devil. The devil hates the spirit of forgiveness not just because of the love that it generates and promotes within the Body that causes us to care and become concerned with well-being of one another (though that would be cause enough for him to hate it), but also because of the level of power and strength that we attain each time we choose to forgive one another. How do we effectively use forgiveness as a weapon?

CHAPTER ONE

FORGIVENESS HAS A BOOMERANG EFFECT

We as beings of flesh and blood feel it deeply when we are wronged and offended by others. We understand the feelings of betrayal, hurt, anger, humiliation, and sadness. Let's face it, some offenses just seem so hard to let go. Some pain seems impossible to release. Some betrayals are hard to get past, particularly if the results of those offenses alter the course you've set for your life. For example, how can God expect you to forgive that spouse that had an affair that has changed and maybe even destroyed the makeup of your family? How can God ask you to forgive that friend that betrayed your trust and caused you to be subject to open humiliation? Surely God cannot require you to forgive those who have lied on you and mistreated you to the point that your character and integrity are put under undo scrutiny. He does require it and He does expect it. And He should!

There is a real truth that we must first admit and then accept about ourselves, and that is that in times past we were the offender. There are people right now that are wounded, broken, and hurting as a result of some encounter with us. We have been guilty of saying or doing the wrong thing too. We use carnal reasoning to justify what we've done by saying to others to get over themselves because you were only joking. We've been guilty of laughing at someone and hurting their feelings or talking about someone in an uncomplimentary way and hoping they don't know it. We have either forgotten or are simply ignoring the commands that God has given us in His word that requires us to become reconciled with our brothers and sisters in Christ, and that we live at peace with our enemies. Therefore, we are indebted to others even though we only want to focus on how others are indebted to us. WE TOO NEED TO BE FORGIVEN! When we forgive others for what they do to us, no matter how difficult it may be, then God forgives us for what we have done to others. In Matthew 6:12 we find Jesus teaching the people to pray. In the prayer He uses the words "as we" indicating a place of exchange. When we refuse to forgive we literally block the avenues of forgiveness we need applied to our own lives. Consider this: God's righteousness and justice are too perfect to only punish those who wrong us, but overlook the wrongs we commit against others. Think of forgiveness as a buffer against the attacks of the devil. Like a boomerang, as we forgive then forgiveness comes back to us (see Matthew 6:14-15). Think of the many things we can do in a day that can be contrary to the will of God. If we have been forgiving to our fellow man then God will forgive us for those things even though we may not be aware that we have done wrong. Having a readiness to forgive keeps us in a place of right standing with God that we can access even when we are unaware that we need to repent of offending someone ourselves. The Bible teaches us that Jesus is our advocate, or simply put, our defense attorney that pleads with God on our behalf when we repent of our wrongs before God. When we are forgiving of others then our forgiveness makes us deserving of forgiveness from God.

Forgiveness Voids The Devil's Power And Increases Our Power

The devil's limited power is rendered void when we forgive. The truth is that the devil's desire is that we remain offended so that it would seem difficult and even impossible to forgive. The question here is why is it so important to the devil that we remain offended? The answer is because forgiveness is like a catalyst that activates the steps of our divine process that will ultimately lead us to our destiny. No one reaches their destiny without going through a process. No process is successful without experiencing both pain and privilege, comfort and challenges, and acquisitions and accusations. If we have trouble with forgiveness then we will have trouble going through the divine process. The devil is going to challenge us at every step of our process to attempt to get us to disobey God. Our disobedience to God gives him some power (we will look at this more closely in the next chapter).

One of the steps in our divine process is known as "positioning." God spoke to me and defined *positioning* as *being placed or situated in circumstances or conditions that will become altered and maybe even transformed by your presence, your talents, and your input.* The most significant thing to remember about positioning is that our cooperation is vital to its success. God will never position anyone who is stubborn and willfully disobeying Him. Allowing offense to remain doesn't just hinder our process towards our destiny; if it remains long enough it will stop the process altogether. It is true that offenses are going to come, we cannot stop them, but we have the power in our hands whether or not we remain offended. The sooner we forgive, the sooner we can start the part of our divine process that will position us and propel us into our destiny. One of the best examples of this in the Bible is that of Joseph (Genesis chapters 36-47). Joseph knew from a very young age that he was destined to be a man of great authority. He knew at some point in his life that people would bow to him and have great respect for him. He even realized that his own family would not be exempt from respecting the authority that he would be granted. When he shared with his family what God showed him concerning his destiny they did not beam with pride or encourage him by offering to help him pursue it. They, instead, became jealous and angry. His own family plotted to kill him. They eventually settled for selling him as a slave. Joseph probably felt betrayed, hurt, humiliated, angry, and even ashamed.

At some point he may have even been tempted to despise his destiny. The words he speaks in Genesis 45:5-8 are so profound when we look at all the offenses he encountered, and all the persecutions that he suffered first at the hands of his own brothers, then by Potiphar's wife, and then to be forgotten by those released from prison to whom he had been a blessing. After he reveals his true identity to his brothers, he in essence tells them not to feel any guilt or shame about what they did to him. He forgave them because he believed that everything that happened to him was orchestrated by God to position him to be a blessing to both the people of Israel and the people of Egypt.

The Word of God teaches us that all things work together for our good (see Romans 8:28). In God's infinite wisdom He will allow us to experience some circumstances that will be adverse or even cruel according to our carnal reasoning. We must mature in our understanding and come to the knowledge that everything, including the hurt and the pain is necessary to usher us into our destinies. We have been taught that God tailor makes blessings for us. This is not entirely true. The truth is God tailor makes us for the blessings. He knows where we are going, and who we are more than we know ourselves. He knows what we need to transition into before He can use us for His service. Joseph understood and accepted that all that happened to him was his process. He could easily forgive his brothers because he did not view what they did to him as mean and despicable, but rather he viewed it as God loving him enough, and trusting him enough to use him this way. Joseph had an understanding about his destiny that we have to come to about our own destinies and that is that God uses these experiences as defining moments and learning experiences. He saw these seemingly unthinkable persecutions as God's way of increasing his wisdom and qualifying him to walk into his destiny. Centuries later we would see our Lord Jesus Christ have the same sentiments as nails were hammered into His hands and feet, and He would be pierced in His side and hung on a cross. We would hear Him say, "Father forgive them..." When we refuse to forgive, our spiritual growth is stunted and our process is hindered. The devil knows that God has a specific assignment that He wants to use only you to fulfill. Fulfilling this assignment will not only bless you but you will be a blessing to others and give God the glory due Him.

When we began the process of entering our destiny we must first answer and then accept our calling. We must understand the "yes" that we say. When we say yes to God we consent to what God has shown us about our destiny thus far. Please grasp this: our process qualifies and justifies us to enter into our destiny, and claim all the blessings that come with it. We are saying yes to allowing God to break us and discipline us. At every junction of the process we must be willing to continue to say yes. Our process, at times, may be difficult and frustrating. It may not always bring us joy, and it may not always make us feel feelings of fulfillment. But if we deny ourselves and embrace our challenges we become worthy to receive from God and be used by Him. It may be difficult to accept, but offense, when it comes, can be useful in helping us to identify our weaknesses and faults. How? By changing the questions we ask ourselves when offenses come. Instead of asking ourselves, "Why did this happen to me?" ask yourself, "Why did I react to what happened to me this way?"

Before going further, please take a moment right now to "selah," that is to meditate and consider these questions:

1. Should you change your perspective of the things that have happened to you and be willing to consider that maybe all that has been done to you was really God shaping, molding, and preparing you to enter your blessed place?

2. Are you willing to embrace the notion that God can use what has happened to you to strengthen your character and fortify your integrity?

If you have carefully considered these questions and answered "yes" to either or both of them, then you must forgive so that the avenues of your destiny and the destinies of those to whom you are assigned to can be fulfilled. You have a deposit within you for the Kingdom of God. Don't allow the devil to hold your deposit hostage because of unforgiveness.

Forgiveness Has Benefits. Unforgiveness Has Consequences.

One of the consequences of unforgiveness is *estrangement, which by definition means to divert in affection or personal attachment. Estrangement also is an arousal of enmity or indifference where originally there had been love, affection, or friendliness.* Forgiveness creates an atmosphere of unity. The devil cannot prevail in an atmosphere of unity and he knows it. By letting go of our feelings of anger and resentment towards each other, and becoming reconciled with each other, we produce an atmosphere of "touching and agreeing" that invites the Spirit of God in our midst (Matthew 18: 18-20). When we speak of touching in this context we are not speaking of physical contact per se; but we are speaking of a focal point where all parties are focused. It becomes an atmosphere where we can relate to each other, understand each other, and embrace each other. It's an atmosphere of unguarded acceptance and total unity. Touching, also, is accepting a portion of the burden that your brothers and sisters are carrying. You become willing to face the same attacks from the devil. This atmosphere binds Satan! This is why he works so hard to keep us from a place of reconciliation. If we forgive each other then we will become reconciled. If we become reconciled we will have the power to touch and agree. If we touch and agree then the Spirit of God will come in our midst. If the Spirit of God comes in our midst then we can ask Him anything we want and He will give it to us.

Unforgiveness is like an invitation asking the devil to come and dwell with you. If the devil is allowed to dwell with you then God cannot. They cannot live together and share the same space. Know this: God "will not" force His way in; you must invite Him. The devil "cannot" force his way in; you must invite him. Notice the invitation is in your hands. Who will you invite? If you are willing to forgive then God will come. If God receives your invitation He will not only open to you avenues of great blessings, but also become a strong fortress against any and all attacks from the devil. If you are not willing to forgive then the devil will come. If you allow the devil to come then you equip him with the devices and the power that he will willingly use against you.

The devil is aware that forgiving each other is one way of "resisting" him, and the power of resistance causes him to take flight. Why? The answer is because he has no power of force. He cannot make you do anything. He has nothing in his arsenal strong enough to defeat you. He knows you are the one to whom God has given the power. You are the one to whom God had given the might. He has to run because he has nothing to fight with. His only hope of getting any victory is when you yield to him. The devil would rather that we never realize that when he was expelled from Heaven he was stripped of everything he had. He has nothing and he never will again. He has no choice. He has to use subtlety and manipulation. Accept this revelation that the devil DOES NOT want to fight you. He wants to avoid all instances of open warfare with you. He is well aware that he is void of power and is already defeated before he even engages in the fight.

He has to stoop to lying and manipulation. Resisting is an act of power and strength. It's a position of force. When he runs, he is retreating. HE MUST YIELD TO YOUR POWER! Don't allow him to manipulate you into thinking that if you forgive a trespass you will appear weak. On the contrary, each act of forgiveness will empower you. We can now understand why Jesus taught Peter don't just forgive your brother seven times but forgive him 70 x 7 times. It becomes clear that we are able to forgive beyond the 7th degree, but we also are able to forgive to the 490th degree. Every offense deserves your forgiveness because you deserve your power, and the devil has earned and deserves his defeat.

CHAPTER TWO

FORGIVENESS IS A MATTER OF THE HEART

Forgiveness, when it is real and sincere, comes from the heart. Unforgiveness creates three devastating effects on your spiritual well-being. It:

1. hardens the heart;

2. contaminates your consecration;

3. annuls your anointing.

Let's look at these three dynamics more closely.

Unforgiveness Hardens the Heart

In the book of Exodus we can see the effects of a hardened heart when we look at the behavior of Pharaoh. Because of the hardness of his heart he was unable to feel compassion. He was unable to sympathize or empathize. Originally, all the Israelites wanted to do was to go to a place to worship the Lord and come back. Pharaoh, however, had developed a sense of distrust and wouldn't allow it. He, instead, enslaved them, increased their work load, gave them less to work with, and required that they produce the same amount of product with less. All this evil reasoning was because of his own distrust. Distrust is a classic symptom of unforgiveness. When we forgive we exemplify "trusting behavior." God requires that we love those who hate us; that we rejoice and celebrate when we are persecuted; that we feed and care for our enemies when we find them in need; and that group that despitefully uses us – those that con us and deceive us to take or exploit what we have without even a thank you; those that have no problem stealing ideas from us then taking credit for your works and not giving you an honorable mention - God says that these people are worthy of our prayers. As hard as it may be to forgive, when we do, we show God how much we trust Him. God expects us to trust Him to handle the situations of offense as He sees best, whether He punishes those who offends us, or whether He chooses to forgive them and bless them in our face. The true test of our trust in God is when we have no understanding of what He is doing, but we agree with Him and follow Him anyway.

Failure to forgive causes us to yield our hearts to the devil who will bring to our hearts a spirit of distrust. Out of distrust comes suspicion. Distrust takes away peace. A heart that does not have peace produces thoughts of retaliation against those who have offended us. The devil gains a victory when he can convince us to retaliate. The ultimate retaliation is holding offenses in your heart. But you are not retaliating against the devil or the one who has offended you. You are retaliating against the will of God. The devil knows that we will never be able to avoid offenses. They are going to come. However, the devil wants us to hold offenses in our hearts because it gives him access to our minds, and thereby, he has access to our ability to reason. If our ability to reason is clouded by offense rather than forgiveness, we will keep reliving those moments when we were devastated and embarrassed. Those feelings of resentment, or hatred, or sadness, or maybe even self loathing will be fresh in our minds every time we are confronted with whomever or whatever offended us. Now it doesn't matter whether the offense happened yesterday or 30 years ago, it still feels the same.

The devil's strategy is to cause us to continue to remember the feelings of our offenses and become hardened to the voice and will of God. He knows that once we experience something it is nearly impossible to forget it. He uses offense to do two things at once. First, he is able to use offense to disrupt our peace. We communicate differently when we have no peace. Even our prayers will reflect that we have no peace. God commands that we pray blessings on those who offend us, but it is impossible to do this if our spirits are full of offense. Part of the assignment of the Body of Christ is to pray without ceasing, and this includes those who may have offended us. How can we expect God to send us to pray for other nations and we cannot pray for our next door neighbor whom we haven't spoken to in months. Secondly, he uses offense to distract our focus from our intended assignments. Even when we spend time praying to get past or forget our feelings of offense, our focus is still shifted and the devil is pleased. The devil will use whatever he can to distract us, even our prayers. There is a level of maturity that the Body of Christ of the 21st century must reach that will enable them to persevere in persecutions and offense. Understand that God is not unconcerned when we are hurt. He will exact vengeance (we will examine this point more closely in chapter three). Consider this: Don't spend time trying to forget those feelings of offense, rather remember them. Just remember them with a different attitude. Remember with the attitude that even though this experience is painful it has to be working together for my good; therefore, I'm going to rejoice over this until I can understand how. I am going to view every offender as an "operative" who has given me tools and information that I need to propel me into my purpose. I will no longer focus on my pain as a reason to question God or my assignment, but I will bear this pain and turn it into the passion I need to motivate me to keep moving. I will no longer cry tears of woe, but tears of joy because I know that this is a part of my divine process.

The next thing we see in these passages in Exodus is that Pharaoh became intimidated by how God had blessed the Israelite's population to grow. He looked at their numbers and began to believe that the Egyptians could be overthrown if there was ever a military takeover. He obviously never took the time to learn about the relationship between the two nations. He saw Israel as a people he had to conquer and control, so he enslaved them. Due to the hardness of his heart he became fearful, and his viewpoints were distorted. Remember that the devil is the author of lies. When your heart becomes hardened then the devil can distort information that is received in the mind. Misunderstandings are birthed out of information that the mind distorts. God's command is that we reason together. This place of reasoning is blessed, not because it always ends in unity due to agreement, but because it always ends in unity due to acceptance. We are not always going to agree with each other. Disagreements don't always have to turn into arguments, and arguments don't have to turn into wars. Disagreements don't always have to be of the devil. A disagreement can be a useful reasoning tool. Disagreements can simply be a case of bringing different pieces of a puzzle together. For example, we can all be striving to accomplish the same thing, but have different viewpoints on how to make it work. The devil will never want us to reason together. Disagreements without offense produce maturity. The devil cannot thrive within misunderstandings if there is a level of maturity that will compel us to communicate with each other. Ask yourself at this point: Could it be that the misunderstanding that I have with a certain person could be cleared up if I would just humble myself and go and reason with him? Is the devil using this to distract me from an assignment that God is trying to give me?

Unforgiveness Contaminates Your Consecration

In Matthew 5:23-24 you find these words, "Therefore if thou bring thy gift to the altar, and there rememberest that thy brother hath aught against thee: Leave there thy gift before the altar, and go thy way; first, be reconciled to thy brother, and then come and offer thy gift." There is an interesting question to consider here. Notice that the one offering the gift has forgotten that there is an unresolved issue between him and his brother. God sees this as a defilement of the gift. God will not accept a defiled gift, so He gives the giver a chance to make his gift acceptable by reconciling with his brother. If God will not allow a gift to be presented to Him due to an innocent act of forgetting an unresolved issue, then why would someone who is well aware of unresolved issues and their own unforgiveness even make an attempt to offer gifts to God? The answer is something that I call "THE CAIN SYNDROME." In the book of Genesis, Cain had the means and the ability to offer God an offering that He could accept, but his attitude defiled his gift. Those plagued by the Cain Syndrome have the attitude that God should take whatever He is offered. They mistakenly focus on what is given rather than the act of giving. The Apostle Paul taught us that we should offer our bodies as living sacrifices unto God, holy and acceptable. The key here is "holy" and "acceptable." We must understand that the value of what we give is solely depended upon the condition we are in when we give it.

When we offer a gift to God we are doing two things: we are worshiping Him, and we are communicating with Him. It is then important that before we attempt to offer anything to God that we make sure our spirits do not contain any contaminates such as unforgiveness. Unforgiveness tarnishes and devalues our gifts, and renders our works useless. When we offer gifts to God without making the attempts to reconcile with our brothers and sisters knowing there are offenses present, then we create an atmosphere where the devil can thrive. Our spirits are then open to the character of the devil and not the character of God. Instead of producing fruits of the Spirit, we exemplify works of the flesh. Some may be asking themselves, "Suppose I go to reconcile with my brother or sister and they still reject me?"

It doesn't matter. The attempt to reconcile is valuable in the sight of God. Why? Because making the attempt is an act of obedience to God. It will not only strengthen your character, it will take you to another level of power over the devil. All too often we try to offer God gifts that we know are defiled. When God gives us a gift He expects us to use it AND take care of it. We are not taking care of the gifts God has given us when we allow offense and unforgiveness to linger in our hearts. If the devil sees that he cannot stop us from using our gifts, then he will attempt to contaminate our gifts. The devil will have us to believe that using our gifts is the principle thing, but it is not. Submitting our gifts to God for His use is really the principle thing. This is what being consecrated is all about. Focus on this fact: God is more concerned with the giver than the gift. Our gifts represent us. The devil is aware that whatever condition we are when we offer our gifts that is the condition the gift is in as well. The devil does not care how much money we give to the church. He doesn't care how often we go to church. He is not impressed with our talents to preach or even prophesy. What puts us on the devil's radar is submitting what we do and what we have for God to use. Submission does not just give God the right to perfect what we do and what we give; it gives Him the right to perfect us.

It is clear then that our gifts have two purposes: they have an intent and they have a directive. When God positions us to use our gifts He does so with a specific assignment in mind. This is what I mean by intent. Understand that when we use our gifts to God's glory He already knows what the outcome will be. He already knows who's going to be blessed and what yokes are going to be broken. You can do what you do with offense and unforgiveness in your heart, but it derails the intentions that God has in His mind because it binds up the anointing that should be released. Your gifts also have a directive, meaning you are positioned to complete a mission. You then are able to become a tool in God's hands because of the gifts that He has given. It is clear that when our gifts operate with God's intentions and directives we are able to build up what God wants and tear down the devil's plans. This is power. Again it is not the gift that is principle, but the power that it is laced with from God who gave it. Harboring offenses and unforgiveness takes the power from the gift. What a wonderful gift Cain had. He was a farmer. He was gifted to bring seed to life and make things grow. He was gifted to provide what was necessary to sustain life in the animals and humans around him. Had he understood the intent and directive of his gift he would have partnered with his brother Abel and accomplished something great in the earth. Instead, he chose to be offended with God for accepting his brother's gift, and with his brother for being in a position where God could accept his gift. The saddest part of this account is not that Cain slew his own brother, but that all he had to do was change his attitude and his gift would have been accepted too. He allowed his offense to drive him to make a terrible choice.

God tried to encourage Cain by telling him that if he would change his attitude then He could accept his offering. I submit that he probably offered God good crops, but because his attitude was so bad God could not respect it. Meaning, he could not receive the blessings he thought he deserved from his offering. From Cain's viewpoint, he had done the same thing that his brother Abel had done, yet Abel received a blessing from God and he did not. This is why the Cain Syndrome is so detrimental. It only allows us to look at what we are doing not at who we are. It drives us to make decisions that we feel compelled to make that we really don't have to. Remember, that even when God can't accept or respect what we may be doing right now, He will always give us a chance to make it respectable and acceptable. Don't choose to walk in offenses and fall victim to the Cain Syndrome.

Let's pause here and do a quick self check. Do you give God a tenth of your increase consistently, and yet you do not see a great change in your financial state, and you don't know why and you complain to God constantly about when your time is coming, and that it is not fair that He is blessing others and not you? Check your attitude. You may be a victim of the Cain Syndrome. Are you working hard on your job or for the church, and it seems that others are getting accolades who, in your opinion, are not contributing as much as you are and you want to quit because you feel you deserve better treatment than you are receiving because you know what you are giving? Check your attitude. You may be a victim of the Cain Syndrome. Don't stop giving! Don't stop working! Just change your attitude.

Unforgiveness Annuls Your Anointing

Accept the fact that the devil does not care how much ability you have. He is not impressed with how much wealth you may acquire. Not even your level of power really concerns him. What does frighten him is your anointing. There are three abilities to the anointing that we will examine: the anointing gives us divine power, the anointing gives us divine approval, and the anointing gives us divine permission.

Divine power speaks not of physical enablement, but a disposition, an attitude that says "I can do all things through Christ that strengthens me." This power is the fuel of our faith that gives us confidence and makes us determined. This anointed power causes us to think strategically. Strategic thinking under divine power exposes what Revelations 2:13 calls Satan's "seat." The word seat in this context is the devil's unexposed position where he is enthroned. It also reveals to us the form that he has transformed himself into. The devil will never work exposed because when we know where he is and what he is trying to do then we can easily defeat him. The devil is well aware of some facts that we seem to easily overlook, and that is that we are wiser, stronger, and mightier than he is. As long as we are focused on obeying God he has no "seat" in our lives. He attempts to be methodical in using his devices to hold us in a place of offense and unforgiveness. His aim is for us to be so focused on the fact that we have been offended, that we forget that we have the power and the right to conquer and subdue what has offended us.

Consider this: offenses can be let go of as quickly and as easily as they come. The devil cannot make us stay in a place of offense. As soon as we let go of offense and forgive, we dethrone the devil and oust him from his seat. Exposing him is bringing him in the light. Whenever he is brought in the light then it becomes obvious how foolish and impotent his deeds are. The most effective way to fight the devil is to develop qualities that will bring light into our hearts. Qualities such as insight, great understanding, and wisdom only come from spending time with God. One way the devil tries to hide himself is behind a cloak of unforgiveness. When we forgive we shatter that cloak and become able to see the devices he is using to hinder us. Listen to this: There is only one way that the devil can gain any power, and it is through our disobedience to God. Our fears do not give him power unless we are so afraid that we disobey God. When we become so afraid that we disobey God, we allow the devil to take a seat in our fear where he will then control us with fear. Every time we try to move towards our destiny he will give us reasons to be afraid. He will do the same thing with offense. Offense does not give the devil power unless we walk in it. The devil is able to take a seat in our offenses and will then try to convince us that we cannot and should not forgive. Now, it is easy to hate without conviction because the devil has a seat called offense that he is ruling from. If we want to oust him from his seat it is not hard at all. All we have to do is expose him by admitting that we have given him a seat, and then tell him to go. He does not want you to know it, but it is that simple. The key is once he leaves fill that seat with God's spirit.

Secondly, God's anointing gives us divine approval. There is no approval rating higher than God's. Divine approval is God's declaration that we are who He says we are. God's aim is to work through us so that we can receive a "well done" in our spirits. It goes without saying that the devil's aim is to keep us from being a pleasure to God. Doesn't it make sense that the devil would want us hold offenses in our hearts towards each other? God is love. You cannot get His approval without knowing how to love the way He loves. We learn to love each other when we communicate with each other. This opens the avenues we need to understanding, accepting, and getting to know each other. Know that to accomplish the will of God in the earth, we will often need to work with someone else. In the corporate world this is known as networking. Networking is not only connecting with the right people, it is a way to strengthen the core of a business by pooling assets of each business together. Through building networks, the corporate world has more of an ability to protect itself from failures and hostile takeovers. Networking can cause a business to expand its assets and successfully diversify.

Connecting in the spirit works the same way. No matter how anointed you are you will need to connect with someone to complete your assignments in the earth. It is how God set up life itself. When we study the creation we find that God designed life that it will only continue when it finds its suitable connection. This is why He created Eve for Adam. They were not just made to procreate, but they were made as a team to have control over everything that God had created. They were made not just to care for the earth, but they were made to control it and set it on a proper course. They were given the command to determine how the earth would function. In Genesis 1:28 you will find the words replenish, which means to provide more or multiply; subdue which means to conquer and assume control; and have dominion over, which means to have power or charge over. This was the ultimate in divine approval! He could trust them to this wise because they were made to be exactly as He was. They were replicas of God. Knowing these facts, it becomes quite clear why the devil works so hard to keep people from connecting with each other.

Remember, that the reason that the devil was expelled from Heaven was because he tried to control God. He could not accomplish it and he, and those who sided with him were quickly expelled. Jesus said that He saw Satan fall like lightning. When Satan beguiled Eve he was not trying to get them kicked out of the garden; he looked at how they functioned and knew they were replicas of God. It was simply another vain attempt to control God. Just like the first time, he, and those who sided with him had to be expelled. Please understand something: when we talk about "the flesh" we are not talking about skin and bones. We are talking about the ungodly nature of a person that the devil was able to deposit because of the disobedience of Adam and Eve. Before the fall, man had a totally divine nature. After the fall, the divine nature did not go away, but we have to constantly deal with this other, demonic nature. Before the fall we were unable to make a bad decision or act in ungodly ways because all of our decision making processes and all of our actions were after a divine or Godly order. After the fall we find that we need to contend with this other nature – the flesh nature. God forgave mankind and sent His only begotten son to give His life so that the flesh nature, that demonic deposit that the devil left in us, could die. It worked! When circumstances arise and we yield to our divine nature then the flesh weakens and eventually will die. Because God forgave mankind and sent him a remedy we are able to resume the assignment that God intended for us in the earth in the first place, which is to replenish, subdue, and have dominion over.

Consider three important actions that take place when we forgive. First, we revert back to what God intended for us when we were created, to be a replica of Him. The Apostle Paul says that it is not robbery to consider yourself equal with God. Having a forgiving attitude is just like God. He is always willing to forgive anyone for anything. Secondly, forgiveness causes our divine nature to grow and become stronger. You don't ever have to wait for anyone to ask for forgiveness. Learn to forgive with or without permission because it is healthy to your spiritual well-being. Forgiveness is so perfect that the one you need to forgive does not have to be present to receive it. They can be dead and still you can forgive them. How? Because forgiveness is a divine maintenance tool that, when you use it, maintains your covenant with God and subdues and controls our ungodly nature. Thirdly, forgiveness pulls down the strongholds that the flesh nature has built. We start to communicate when we forgive, not just with each other, but with God. Communication on this level has a transforming effect because now God can reveal those deep things that He wants to tell us anyway. God loves it when we talk to Him and He loves talking to us. We know how communication builds relationships. Talk to Him like you would a friend.

Thirdly, God's anointing grants divine permission. Divine permission brands the "go" in your spirit. When God grants us divine permission He is giving us a nod to work in His name and on His behalf. He equips us with what we need to carry out every assignment. If we don't know how to be forgiving then we cannot be sent by God to do anything for Him. The devil understands a revelation about our assignments that we do not and that is that the function of the assignment is not the principle thing. What is key is something called "transference." This is how it works: each time God gives us an assignment we are acting as His representatives. We are giving Him permission to use our bodies. Thus, we allow Him to use our mouths, our hands, and our feet. Therefore, as we do what He has told us to do it is really not us, but Him doing the work. He can then transfer into the earth what is needed to come from Him. Let's look at an example to make this more understandable. Let's say that God has gifted you musically. Each time God wants to transfer hope, or healing, or knowledge, or break a demonic yoke, He will create an opportunity for your gift to be used. All He wants you to do is be ready and surrendered when He is ready to use you. All you have to do is align to His will and to those He will connect you with to bring His will to pass. It may shock you to know that the devil really doesn't care who you like and dislike or who you choose to be friends with. He is only concerned with alliances and relationships that God can use to transfer and release from God what is needed to transform society more into the image of God.

Here are some challenges to consider. Think about that co-worker that you don't like and seem to only feel antagonism towards. Could it be that the devil is using these feelings of antagonism to keep you from becoming allies? To become allies the two of you together may be used by God to transfer into the atmosphere of that job a concept that will bless the whole workplace? Forgive and find out! Or think about that brother or sister at the church that you attend that you just cannot seem to get along with. Could it be that they are the very ones you need to jump start a ministry that God will use to bring help and hope not just to the church but to the surrounding community? Forgive and find out! And what about that person who has wounded you so deeply that you feel that you may never recover. Could it be that God has given to them the deposit you need to receive to take you to the next step in the process of fulfilling your destiny? Forgive and find out!

Using Forgiveness as a Weapon of Warfare

CHAPTER THREE

DON'T TAKE THINGS SO PERSONALLY... GOD ALREADY DOES!

Allow me to paint a picture right here if you will. You are a child who has to deal with a bully everyday. This bully taunts you, teases you, humiliates you, and tries to intimidate you all the time. It would seem that his only mission in life is to make your life as miserable as he can. You take it for a while because you feel powerless to stop him. But then one day with tears in your eyes you decide to tell your father about your ordeal. Your father reassures you and says to you, "Come on. I'm going to teach you how to fight this bully." In the same way, only God can teach us how to defend ourselves against the wiles and attacks of the devil. God is a God of mercy. But He also is a God of justice. When it is time to defend His children He does not hesitate to come and rescue them. He knows how to fight and He will not hesitate to fight against any enemy who tries to harm His children. He's a father who not only will fight for His children He will teach his children how to fight. He will give them weapons to use and show them how to use them. He knows there are bullies out here who will always try to attack us so He has defenses already in place that will gain us victory as we fight. The key is we must learn to fight with the weapons He gives us His way. The word of God declares that these weapons are mighty to the pulling down of strongholds.

No matter how many people you learn to love or how many people you vow to help you will still have enemies. God is aware that there are people who we will come into contact with that are going to hurt us. They will take pleasure in humiliating us. They will enjoy lying on us. They want to see us fall and will do their part in making sure that it happens. God requires that we even love and forgive these people, not because He is overlooking their behavior, but because He wants us to let Him handle it. He declares that vengeance is His and He will repay. In Isaiah 54: 17 the word teaches us that "no weapon formed against us will prosper..." Notice that it didn't say that no weapons would be formed. Weapons will be formed but they will not prosper. This does not mean that we will not have to face and handle some adverse situations. This does not mean that we won't ever have to face difficulties. It does let us know that those situations that the devil thought would damage us beyond repair can ultimately be the very thing that catapults us into our destiny. God desires that our behavior change towards our enemies. Each mistreatment towards you must be countered with well treatment from you. Actually, enemies are vital components to your spiritual well-being. One way that God defends us is that He makes them footstools (Psalm 110:1). Footstools are portable steps used for mounting onto higher places. They are used to bring the additional height needed to comfortably step up to a place you need to climb onto. God is able to transform the works of enemies to the extent that who the devil intended to use to bring you down, will instead give you the step up necessary to go into the next level of your destiny. To activate the power of this defense mechanism we must not only forgive our enemies, but pray blessings on them.

The tactics of enemies are only detrimental to us when we succumb to the effects of the attacks. When we learn the value of rejoicing during and after the attacks we will find the attacks rich sources of blessings. Enemies, many times, are the ones who ultimately usher us into our purpose and help us fulfill our destiny. Jesus said about Judas, "I chose him and I know he is going to betray me (John 13:18). As we study the ministry of Christ, notice that there were many times that attempts were made to capture Him, but He was always able to escape in the crowds. It wasn't until His confidant, His friend, His disciple betrayed Him that the final steps of His purpose were accomplished. Judas' betrayal was fundamental in bringing Christ to the threshold of His purpose. We find forgiveness hard because we feel the sting of offense. It's normal human emotion to react to offense with resentment and anger. God does not condemn us for these reactions unless we refuse to take the proper steps to release these emotions. He knows that if we hold these emotions in our hearts they will damage us and defeat us. We have to learn how to get pass the pain to see the purpose. God teaches to rejoice when we are persecuted. Let's look at three main reasons why.

1. Rejoicing During Persecution Gives Us Insight

(See Romans 8:28). The act of rejoicing opens our understanding as to why we are being attacked. When we understand why we are being attacked, then we can accept that we are being attacked, and the attack won't discourage us. Insight will reveal to us the good in the attack. Believe it or not, in every attack there is a valuable nugget that we need. It may be a deeper anointing. It may be more wisdom or knowledge. It may be more maturity. But we are gaining something. God would not allow the devil to attack us for his own pleasure. He will never stand idly by and watch the devil inflict pain on us in vain. God loves us too much for that. He will, however, allow us to go through whatever is necessary to make us what He would have us to be. Think of the attacks as a chisel cutting away those attributes in us that are not like God. Those attributes that, left unchecked, will result in the works of the flesh. Attacks can be diversions and distractions that the devil uses to take our focus away from where God is leading us. It is his hope that each time we try to move towards the will of God we will remember the pain we felt and become discouraged. His demonic aim is to use the pain of the attack to debilitate us. If we become debilitated then even when we would want to move we won't be able to. Either we will be too afraid to move, or too discouraged to move. However, if we can just obey God and rejoice and be exceedingly glad we will associate joy with the attack rather than pain. Insight brings light. Light is revelation. Light is knowledge. Light is understanding. The devil hates all the attributes of light. Darkness is ignorance. The devil can hide in darkness. When light comes, he has no place to hide. When we understand the purpose behind anything it makes it easier to accept the bad with the good. Think of it this way: good athletes put their bodies through rigorous exercises and restrictive diets to maintain their stamina while playing. They have an understanding that this may not be the most pleasant thing to do, but it is necessary to do if they want to perform well. As God's children we must embrace the fact that some attacks are needful to our success. When we embrace this it won't bring dread, it will cause joy. Jesus is our ultimate example of this. Nothing could have been harder to endure than to be nailed to a cross. Yet, the Bible says He endured the pain and humiliation of the cross because He looked in the future and saw the glory of us being reconciled to God. He felt that we were worth it.

2. When We Rejoice During Attacks it Puts Things in their Proper Perspective

Rejoicing helps us accept an attack as a preparing. The root of prepare is *pre* which means before and *pare* which means to cut out or cut away. We now have an understanding of the pare portion of prepare. Yes, we now know that there are issues that need to be eliminated from our lives before we can enter our destiny, and that these issues will hinder and hurt us if not expelled from our lives. Preparation does not just deal with what is eliminated, but also with what is received beforehand. There are character traits that God wants to develop in us before we walk into our destiny. He allows some attacks to occur to discipline us. Discipline is not used to deprive us of anything, rather, it is valuable in developing and building us up. Having things in their proper perspective is seeing the value and importance of something as it relates to what is happening or could happen. If we would take the time to put attacks in their proper perspective we will find that sometimes the attacks buffet us. Buffeting is a good way to achieve discipline and bring about self-control. God has the right to temper us and He will use whatever means He deems fitting. God can stop any attack He wants to, but He can use any attack He wants to as well. Putting attacks in their proper perspective releases the attitude of forgiveness in the atmosphere. Jesus taught us to rejoice and be exceedingly glad. Exceeding gladness is more than just happy; it is celebration. He is actually asking us to celebrate being offended. Understand that there are certain behaviors that manifest themselves when we celebrate. A celebration is a public display of joy. When we celebrate we bring attention to what has made us happy. We do memorials and pay homage to what has brought us joy. This is important to note, that celebrations mark accomplishments. When He is asking us to be exceedingly glad about being persecuted, He is asking us to commemorate an event that has caused a great accomplishment in our life.

The devil will have us believe that when we go through our attacks that we have suffered loss. Not only have we suffered loss, but we have to be offended with the one that we believe has caused us to suffer the loss. God says this is not true. The truth is not only have we not suffered any loss, but we have reached a milestone. Each milestone helps us build up the kingdom of God, and fortify ourselves against the attacks of the devil. Jesus declared that when we are persecuted our reward in heaven becomes great. So think of it this way: every time the devil uses someone to attack or offend you he is actually causing an increase in your heavenly account! His vain attempt to steal, kill, and destroy, is really increasing you, giving you abundance, and building you up. Why wouldn't this make us happy and bring great joy? The devil cannot bring depression when we are celebrating.

3. Rejoicing Releases Healing Virtue

When the devil attacks us, there is no question that he, at the very least intends to wound us. Wounds, especially if they are deep, leave scars. Scars are evidence that there had once been an injury to a particular area. Scars are also evidence of healing. When God heals us, He heals us to the extent that what was an area of intense pain and discomfort is no more. He doesn't just stop at making you feel better, he makes you whole. Wholeness is synonymous with soundness. When something is considered sound it is complete, valid, trustworthy, and showing good judgment. Our joy acts as a balm and a binding. Balms contain ingredients that promote healing and ease pain. The one thing that our flesh finds hard to release after an offense is the pain. Pain does not just manifest itself physically but pain manifests itself emotionally and mentally as well. Pain is not comfortable and pain is not pleasant. When people experience extreme pain they cannot think or act rationally. The devil uses pain as a controlling device. As long as we hold on to the pain of offense he can control us. When we choose to rejoice because of our offenses rather than languish in pain and unforgiveness, we send the message to the devil that we will not be distracted from our assignment and we are well aware of who we are in the Lord.

Bindings are used to restrict movement to prevent further damage. They hold the limb in place until the limb is restored and can move properly. Even if we become broken after we have been attacked by the devil, rejoicing will bring restoration. When a limb is broken it cannot be used. It must be set and bound, and there must be adequate time for it to remain in this state. Continuing to hold on to the pain of offense while trying to minister in any capacity is like trying to use a broken limb as though nothing is wrong with it. There is such a stark contrast between a broken thing and a whole or sound thing. Yet, we often try to function broken the same way we did when we were sound. The only one who gets victory and prospers here is the devil. More often than not it is God that will allow things to happen that will break us, but we can only get victory when we learn to forgive and rejoice as God has commanded.

Even though rejoicing will heal us it does not always remove the scars. When Jesus appeared to the disciples after the crucifixion they did not recognize Him. It wasn't until after they saw His scars that they recognized the one who had walked with them and taught them for three years. Don't be ashamed or embarrassed by your scars. Wear them as trophies of triumph and evidence of effectiveness. Your scars are proof of your soundness.

Though God commands that we rejoice and celebrate when we are attacked, do not think that He overlooks it or is unconcerned when His children are attacked by the devil. In Luke 17:1-2, Jesus declares that offenses are going to come. There is no way around them. But He also declared that woe to him through whom those offenses come. Woe is a state of misery and sorrow. It is misfortune. In essence He is saying do not mess with one of mine. If you do, you've messed with me, and I take it personally.

As loving, merciful, and even forgiving as God is, He is also a God of justice. His justice brings order. His justice is not tainted by emotions. We must realize that when God exacts vengeance He does not act in a spirit of malice or even retribution as we would, but He always moves in such a way that redemption is possible. It is not His will that any should perish in their sins. He sent His son to die for the sins of the whole world. Understand this very important fact: We find it hard to forgive because we judge every offender by flesh, blood, and personality. We say, "Look at what he or she did to me." God is not superficial like this. He judges offenders by looking at their heart, mind, and spirit. Let's look more closely at this. When He looks at their heart He looks at the contents of their heart. By knowing what has entered their heart He knows the "why." He sees the real intent. He knows the real motivation. The real intent and motivation may not have originated out of an evil heart, but a hurt and confused one. They may be afraid and insecure, and their actions may simply be a mask over what they view as a flaw in themselves that they do not want exposed. We react to the manifested behavior, not to the real intents and motivations of the heart. When we forgive them we release God's spirit to minister to their needs not to retaliate against their behavior. This why He asks us to feed them when they are hungry, clothe them when them are naked, and pray for them when they have needs.

God also looks at the beliefs in the offenders mind. By knowing what the mind has accepted as true is the "what." If the contents of the heart are impure, then the thoughts of the mind will also be impure. Our actions and behaviors are results of our beliefs. If the devil is able to enter the heart then he can speak to the mind. If the offender accepts what enters his mind then the devil can dictate the behavior. At this point it does not matter how deviant the suggestions are that the devil may request, it will be acted on. Judas was a chosen disciple, but once the devil entered his heart, telling him to betray Christ made perfect sense. We must also remember that more often than not we act on offenses that we think have happened, not what actually happened. This is why attempts at reconciliation are so important. We must learn to humble ourselves and admit that there have been times we misunderstood the meaning of an action or a comment that has been made. We have acted in error because of what we thought happened. The devil is able to operate with great ease in this case because we are surrendering our peace and joy to a lie. After all, he is the author and father of lies. Choosing to act on our ability to come together and reason together empowers us and weakens the devil.

Also, God looks at the spirit of the offender. Looking at how the spirit is led is the "who." In Matthew 5:12 as Jesus is exhorting us to rejoice over our persecutions He refers to a group that He identifies as "they." He says that they were persecuting saints during the days of the ancient prophets. Who are "they" that He is referring to? They are not flesh and blood, but they are evil spirits sent from the devil to attack the people of God. When the devil led the uprising in Heaven and had to be expelled, a host of angels took the devil's side and had to be expelled along with him. They have been condemned and they have no chance of reconciling with God. They are many, and they are aimless. They are looking for a place to inhabit. They hate God and everything that God loves. They will never be able to repent and be forgiven; therefore, they do not want you to be able to either. They have no real power of force, meaning they can't make you do anything, but they assume control over any body that will yield its members to them (Roman 6:11-13). God is pleased when He can count us worthy to suffer for His sake. When we forgive our offenders then we show the devil that we know that these attacks are really coming from him and the evil spirits that he employs, and that we are holding him responsible. We let the devil know we are not going to wage war against the one who is offending us unawares, but we are going to wage war against him. If you really want to upset the devil, let him know that you intend to love this offender and forgive them to the extent that the love of God in you will draw them away from him to the knowledge of Christ.

God has so many remedies He has given to help us to recover from offenses. Remember, this is a spiritual fight against principalities, powers, the rulers of darkness and spiritual wickedness in high places (Ephesians 6:12). As with any warfare we have to receive instructions from the one who is in control and gives the commands. God is the one who is in control, and He instructs us by His spirit. He sends us out as sheep among wolves, but He does not send us out without protection and the necessary safeguards.

Here are a few instructions that God has given to vindicate us as well as help us recover from offenses.

Shake the Dust From Your Feet

The significance of this instruction has to do with our feet. Two things to note: God has outfitted our feet for warfare with shoes that are prepared with the preparation of the gospel of peace (Ephesians 6:15). No matter what situations we may step into, the deposit that God has given us will usher in His presence. Where His presence is He brings freedom and peace. If we find ourselves in a place and are made welcomed, then God is welcomed there. The spirit of the Lord is free to move and to meet every need in that place. On the other hand, if we are made unwelcomed, the spirit of the Lord is also made unwelcomed. The devil is then given the right to control that place. Every demonic and chaotic spirit is then free to function however it pleases.

Next, God has promised that everywhere our feet tread He will give us that place as an inheritance. It is important to understand here that to give does not always mean to take ownership of. Often God imparts to us a standard that allows us to acquire favor with those who have great power, wealth, and influence. He may not physically give us the ownership of the territory per se, but He grants us such a level of influence that we can have power and influence over the one who does have physical ownership. We saw this happen with Joseph. The spirit of prosperity and preservation is released because we are given the freedom to operate in the power of the Lord, and give this territory to God and give Him charge over it through us. In this sense we have been given this territory. In other words it will not be important to be the CEO when we can find favor and influence the CEO. Shaking the dust is a testimony or declaration that God's presence is no longer here and will never be again. This place is now void of anything that will cause it to prosper and thrive. Now, God has contempt for this place, and redemption is highly unlikely. He is now so displeased with this place that He does not even want the residue of this place on your feet. Shaking the dust is God's way of saying that if this place is not worthy of you, then it is not worthy of me. Any place that is not worthy of God will not survive.

Heap Coals of Fire on Your Enemy's Head

There are actions that we are to do that show that we are forgiving. We are asked to feed our enemy if we find him hungry and give him something to drink if we find him thirsty. Even pray God's blessings on him when we know he has despitefully used us. This seems very strange doesn't it? The word teaches us that when we do this it is like heaping coals of fire on the head of our enemy. Actually, heaping coals of fire is a term of empowerment. When you return an act of hate with an act of love it gives you the power. It puts you in control of the situation. All attacks on us are designed to put us in a vulnerable state where it will be easy for the devil to stifle us and weaken us. Negative attitudes towards us are suppose to discourage us and overshadow the assignments we have been given. Acts of kindness and forgiveness help us to overcome. We can only declare we are overcomers and more than conquerors when we can find the strength within us to fight the urge to desire vengeance. Being a blessing to those who have offended us releases us from feeling an obligation of trying to defend ourselves, and it releases the offender from the obligation they feel to continue to offend. It puts them in the position where their acts of offense are exposed, and thereby exposes the contents of their character and yours. The true measure of power lies not in who can exert the most strength, but in who can exercise the most restraint.

Preparing a Table in the Presence of Your Enemy

This is an act of vindication. God ALWAYS vindicates His children. God will never allow the devil to spread propaganda about Him or His children that He will not prove to be false. The trick here is to totally trust God to do the vindicating. He will vindicate, but in His time and in His way. The devil will have us believe that we need to act on our own behalf. He will cause us to become overly anxious and frustrated in the will and timing of God. But if we can just trust God and be patient with Him and wait for Him then He will bring us to those places of honor.

CHAPTER FOUR

WHY IS FORGIVENESS SO HARD?

There are several reasons why forgiveness is so hard.

There is a Humiliation Factor

When we forgive, we must humble ourselves. To humble yourself is to take the lower or base position. People argue and fight because each party involved is trying to maintain a certain position. The devil knows that God hates pride, so he constantly challenges us by bringing to our flesh the feelings that humility is a position of weakness and fear. Know that when you do humble yourself and forgive, it is not another human you are taking the lesser position to; it is actually the person of the Spirit of God.

The devil does not want you to bow down to the Spirit of God, so he causes your flesh to wrestle with Him. When you don't love your enemy you are wrestling with God. When you don't do good to them that hate you, you are wrestling with God. Don't let the devil trick you into believing that you have the right to defend yourself against an offense. He doesn't care about you being offended, he just wants to prevent you from humbling yourself. He knows when you humble yourself you will be exalted. When you are ready to forgive it puts you in a position of bowing down. The devil knows as long as you are bowing down he cannot plant seeds of pride in your heart; and thereby making it hardened.

There is No Guarantee that Forgiveness Will Stop the Offense

When an individual's spirit is closed or their heart has become hardened there is no guarantee that your acts of kindness will change any of that. There is no guarantee that a good and positive relationship will occur because you forgave them or tried to reconcile with them. It's okay! Forgiveness is something that you do as unto the Lord. The principle of forgiveness is so perfect that it doesn't matter whether the one you are trying to forgive receives you or not, they cannot stop God from blessing you. Please catch this revelation: The ultimate truth is the only real part they play is that they offended you and put you in the place where you could forgive them and get blessed. You are actually able to use them as a catalyst needed to get to the next blessing you are due!

Forgiveness May Reveal the Thorn in Your Flesh

Everyone has areas in their lives that they need to change or allow to die altogether. All of us wrestle with something that we don't put on public display. Sometimes we find that we need to forgive others, not because they did any wrong to us, but because they put us certain positions that shed a spotlight on what we attempted to hide. In this case we are offended by the truth. It is hard to hear revelations about us when we don't believe that what is revealed is putting us in the best light. But if we can accept what we hear it will cause us to grow up in Christ. To grow properly we have to be encouraged to continue in the things that are good and right, and discouraged to continue in the things that are wrong. If you cannot accept the truth about yourself, then the devil can stunt your spiritual growth. We cannot transform into the image of Christ without growing up. Consider the behavior of children when they are offended in some way. They throw tantrums. They become stubborn and stiff. They try to reason their way out of their wrong. They cry a lot to get attention. This is what God sees in an immature saint. There are some things that God is going to allow to happen to us to grow us up. He will not appoint or use an immature saint.

We Find the Act of Release Difficult

One common phrase that we hear from others when we are trying to forgive others is "just let it go!" or "just get over it." The real truth is to release something is a process, not a reflex. As much as we may like to, we can't just get over it. We will have to process our way through the hurt, the pain, and the anger. I submit that the process of releasing has four steps. The first step is to assess. Romans 8:28 explains that "all things work together for the good of those who love God and are the called according to His purpose." The word good here translates to mean benefit or beneficial. To properly assess why we are suffering through this offense we must not ask ourselves why this happened to hurt us, but what benefit will I receive because of this. Every offense yields a benefit! The key is to seek God to find out what is that benefit. Before we can go forward into our assignments there will things about us we must master as well as conquer. We can not master or conquer what we will not confront. We must grasp an understanding that God will not allow anything to happen to us that will not yield some benefit to us. The challenge will be to make the assessment that it is not important that the devil designed what you are going through to hurt you, BUT that God allowed it to bring you some benefit.

The second step is engagement. To engage is to confront. One of the greatest challenges that humans face is how to master what we find painful. We avoid pain because it hurts. No one who considers themselves wise will purposefully walk into a situation that will cause them pain. Unfortunately, we all have been hurt by someone. How was it handled? Unchecked offenses fester like an opened wound. This is another reason why God requires that we attempt to reconcile with each other and forgive each other. Offenses that are not confronted will turn into hatred and malice. Now our spirits are contaminated, the devil has an opening into our hearts, God is not pleased, and our blessings are hindered.

Step three is liberty. Once we assess and confront, it sets us on a path to freedom. We cannot declare freedom until our hearts and minds are free. Unforgiveness holds us in places where we cannot receive the fullness of God's blessings. Jesus says that if He sets you free then you will be free indeed. The word "indeed" here is derived from a Hebrew word which means altogether or also. Jesus is letting us know when we allow Him to free us then He is ushering us into a place of total freedom. Not just freedom from pain and strongholds, but also the freedom to be, the freedom to achieve, the freedom to conquer and dominatate. He is also letting us know that just as He is free so can we be free. Nothing could hold or hinder Him. Not even death. We can have this same strength of freedom!

The final step is forward moving. Once we become free then we can move forward and release these feelings of unforgiveness. What has happened TO US won't carry as much weight as what must happen THROUGH US.

The Justice Files

We believe we are entitled to justice when we are offended. Our sense of justice demands vindication. We want to know that those who have offended us will experience as much pain or even more pain than we are. We believe that this is the only fair way. We count forgiveness as a way of letting them off the hook. We begin to reason within ourselves that if we forgive our offenders then we will appear weak and frightened, and that we are giving them considerations that they have not earned and do not deserve. They have hurt us and they must pay! This is called being vengeful. To be honest these feelings are very understandable. The problem is, however, to be able to justifiably exact vengeance we must be all knowing! When God exacts vengeance He is not just punishing a wrong, He is restoring order. God knows how to set things in order. When He sets things in order it causes recovery and restoration. Consider that God's whole plan of salvation is based on one main thing – forgiveness. Eye for an eye and tooth for a tooth would be fine if the results following would bring order and cause restoration.

Only when we understand the depths of John 3:16 can we fully understand what we have access to. Not only did God provide us with a perfect, unblemished sacrifice in the person of His only Son Jesus; He offered it up for us Himself in such a way that He would be sure to accept it. Imagine being in so much debt that you will never be able to pay, and someone cares for you so much that they take their resources and pay all your debts! This is what God did for us. Not only did God give us the power to be forgiven for our sin debt to Him, but He also gave us the power to forgive others. There is a reason why the devil hates forgiveness so much. He will never experience it! His condemnation is final and his fate is sealed. The devil will never be restored or reconciled to God. He will never ever know what it is like to be forgiven.

Each time we use our weapon of forgiveness we remind the devil just how condemned and defeated he is. There is great hope for us, but there is no hope for him. The devil is like a spoiled brat that says, "If I can't have forgiveness then I am going to do all I can to make sure you can't have it either!" Thanks be to God we can have it if we want it and there is absolutely nothing that the devil can do to stop it.

Using Forgiveness as a Weapon of Warfare

CHAPTER FIVE

GOD HAS FORGIVEN YOU. NOW YOU MUST FORGIVE YOURSELF.

The greatest challenge in the process of forgiving can be, and often is, the challenge of forgiving yourself. We become accustomed to walking under clouds of guilt and wrapping ourselves in shrouds of condemnation. The problem is we want to be free but we feel we don't deserve to be free, and don't understand how to free ourselves. We cannot escape ourselves and that can be torment when we don't like ourselves. One of the most liberating statements God made to me was this: "No weapon formed against you shall prosper even if YOU form the weapon with your own hands!" God has forgiven us and He wants us to enjoy being forgiven. BUT how do we go about forgiving ourselves?

1. Understand that forgiveness is our innate right

We were born in sin and shaped in iniquity, this is true, but we were also born with the right to be forgiven for every wrong, sin, and mistake we have made and will ever make. It is our inalienable right! Meaning it cannot be separated from us or taken from us. Think of it as a birthright because it is. This could be the number one reason that the devil hates us. God's forgiveness is so perfect that He forgives us when we repent and He also forgives us when we don't know to or want to repent. He has even forgiven the sins and trespasses that we haven't committed yet. What a blessing the Father has given us that no matter what mistakes we make forgiveness is waiting on us. All He requires of us is to accept it. The problem is we are so intent on showing God we are sorry, we neglect to exemplify the fruits of forgiveness like peace, confidence, and joy. Know this: God is not condemning you.

God is not holding anything over your head. He said that He has forgotten about it and cast it as far as the east is from the west so that it won't condemn us anymore. He is not the one who keeps bringing it back to your remembrance.

Rejoice in this blessing: Once we repent, God wants us, as a matter of fact He expects us, to act like the breach never happened! It is the devil who is still accusing you, not God. It is the devil who wants you to still feel guilty, not God. It is the devil who is condemning you now, not God. Remember the devil will never experience the joy or the power of being forgiven. When we forgive others and ourselves we open an avenue of blessings that usher us into an even deeper relationship with God. The devil knows that continuing to embrace guilt and condemnation means that the avenues to freedom will continue to be blocked. Let's face it; we can't feel guilty and happy at the same time. We can't feel condemned and joy at the same time. We are productive, more creative, and useful to others and ourselves when we are happy and content. If the devil wants to shut us down then he has to be successful in making us continue to walk in guilt and condemnation. If the devil wants us to believe that we have no value or worth to anyone, then he must find ways to keep us feeling guilty and condemned. WE ARE NOT GUILTY OF ANYTHING. THEREFORE WE SHOULD NOT FEEL CONDEMNED! This is not a statement of pride. It is a statement of truth. Once we repent of our sins and trespasses then we are free. When we allow the Spirit of God to dwell in us and control us then we are free. Once we believe this and truly embrace this then our focus will change from the mistakes that we have made to the possibilities of success and the potentials within us. Our true identities will emerge when we forgive ourselves and operate in our forgiveness. This scares the devil to no end.

2. You must understand what it means to have an advocate with the Father

We quote this passage of scripture all the time (I John 2:1). However, do we really understand what the blessings of advocacy gives to us? Yes, an advocate defends us much like a lawyer does in court. But an advocate also campaigns for a cause. Think about it. While you are asking God for blessings, Jesus Christ is campaigning for you to receive the blessings too, especially when we need Him to forgive us. God will ALWAYS forgive those who ask. I know it seems elementary, but it is just this simple. Jesus sacrificed His life so that we can be forgiven for our sins. When we can't forgive ourselves then we dishonor, disrespect, and disregard the sacrifice that Jesus made for us. God saw us as a cause worth this great sacrifice. (John 3:16). If God sees us as worthy then why don't you see yourself as worthy? An advocate does more than defend wrongs, they also counsel and recommend. When we can't forgive ourselves then we deny ourselves the counsel and directions of the Holy Spirit. You can't hear clearly from the Holy Spirit when your understanding is clouded by condemnation. Even if you hear a word from the Lord your actions will exemplify your feelings of guilt, and this will cause fear and distrust; and this is exactly where the devil wants you to be. Confidence is an attribute of freedom. Our advocate Jesus Christ gives us confidence that we can trust the Father.

Finally, there are two things to remember. First, we must accept that forgiveness is not earned. We did not earn it, and those who we forgive probably won't earn it either, but we do deserve it. How can I say that? Because of what Jesus did on the cross! Second, God sees us as worth forgiving. He didn't just forgive us one time, but He continues to forgive every mistake we make, every bad decision we make, and every act of disobedience we commit. All that He requires is that we ask Him for it. The devil cannot stop us from being forgiven or from forgiving anyone else. When we operate in forgiveness and love as God would have us to do then we reduce the devil into what he really is...HELPLESS AND DEFEATED!

The victory of any warfare is to render your enemy helpless and defeated. Forgive those you need to forgive. Ask for forgiveness from those you need to ask and watch the overwhelming amount of peace that will overtake you the minute you do. You have a right to your blessings. It doesn't matter what you have done, or what state you may be in when you read this book; you are still precious to God and He still considers you one of His. DO NOT forfeit or exchange your weapon of forgiveness another minute. It takes a very strong person to forgive someone. It takes a very brave person to ask for forgiveness. If you want to know if you are using your weapon of forgiveness effectively there is a two-pronged forgiveness test that we can use as a spiritual gage to test our spirits to know if we are forgiving or not. The first prong of the test is this: When you hear of your offenders getting blessed and you don't feel a little resentment towards them. Rather, you agree that they deserve to be blessed and you truly praise God for blessing them while you wait for Him to bless you. Then you have forgiven. The second prong is when you hear of a hardship, problem or downfall of your offenders and you don't gloat and feel pleasure at the expense of their pain. Instead, you pray for their restoration and you offer aid to them when you can. Then you have forgiven. KEEP TAKING THIS TEST UNTIL YOU PASS IT!

To contact the author for speaking engagements, conferences, book tours and book signings in your church or organization, write or call:

SCV Enterprises

Phone:
(336) 355-1165

Website:
www.forgivenessisaweapon.com

Email:
scvinson@aol.com

Other Authors by
DMI PUBLISHING HOUSE

I'm T.O.U.G.H is a 60 day devotional book intended to resolutely ground the reader in a strong spiritual foundation. The messages in this book thrust the reader to think and reflect on their own lives and situations and to dig deep in themselves and be contingent on the victor that is in each and every one of us. Through scriptures, stories, personal testimonies, and teachings, readers will grasp hold to the fact that they are built to last.
ISBN: 978-0-6922-0263-0

For more information, visit
www.imtoughdevotional.com